SLAY! THE DRAGON Presents...

Pink Cloud Poetry

POEMS FROM EARLY RECOVERY

WRITTEN AND ILLUSTRATED BY
GREGORY C WILDER JR.

D1509769

Printed in the United States of America

First Printing, 2020

ISBN 9798640995701

Independently published

https://www.facebook.com/slayyythedragon/

THIS POETRY HAS
NOT BEEN MODIFIED
TO FIT YOUR PC CULTURE

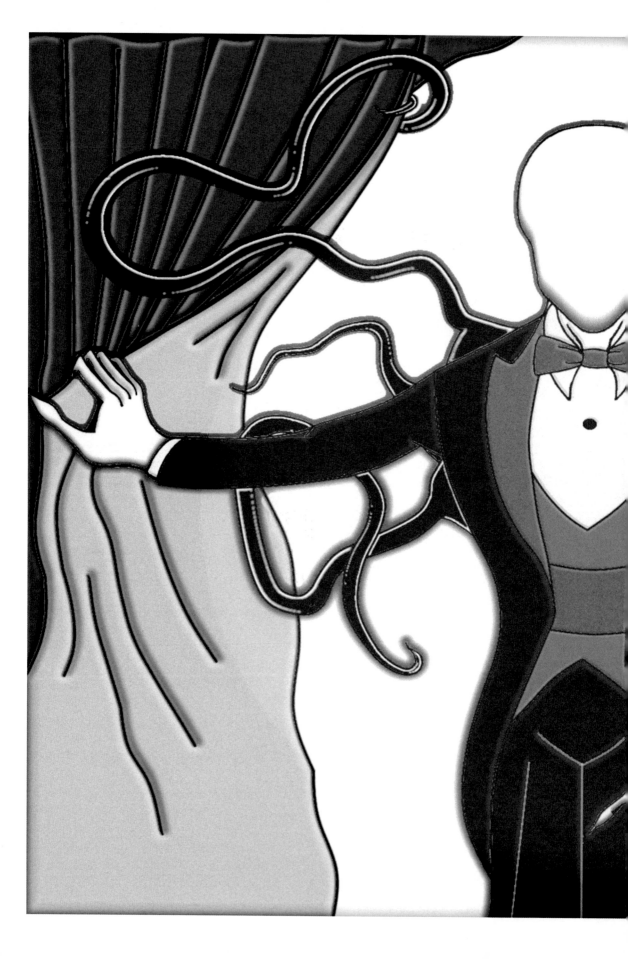

How do you do?
Mr. Wilder feels it would be a little unkind
to present this production without just a
word of friendly warning...
We are about to unfold the story of the
Dragon.
A person of poetry.
Who sought to create profound works of art
in their own image, without reckoning upon
God.
It is one of the strangest tales ever told...
I think it will thrill you. It may shock you.
It might even — make you put down your
smart phones, pull your heads out of your
asses, and actually THINK for a moment!
So if any of you feel that you do not care to
subject your nerves to such a strain, now's
your chance to —
Well... We've warned you.

Gregory C. Wilder Jr. PRESENTS:
A UNIVERSAL MONSTER

A Big Budget Horror Flick: $15 a Bag, 100 a Bundle.
One too many, a thousand never enough.
A long night in the ER,
After drunken cocaine stupor fall from rooftop.
The Fentanyl having no effect at all.
Tolerance, too high… As was I.
The first try unsuccessful,
The Doctor having to re-**SNAP** my arm
To set it back the right way...
But you know what they say:
"*A GOOD CAST IS WORTH REPEATING*".
A shock back from the dead, by Police Narcan shot,
To this fresh corpse in the front seat of my mother's car –

IT'S ALIVE! ALIVE!

Man, What a Time to Be Alive –
Even though

I LOVE DEAD... HATE LIVING.

Wise in my generation – A modern Prometheus
In this world of Gods and Monsters.
So I ask myself: Am I really a Monster?
Or just the sum of all these parts that are not my own?
And run by this abnormal brain – this criminal brain.
But all-the-while still innocent, somewhat clumsy
And just misunderstood. Just looking to fit in.
Following command – Chugging down cups with a

"DRINNNNK GOOOOD"

Just looking for a

FRIEEENNNNDDD.

But leave it to society always mistaking you
For what it was that created you.
This society with its mob mentality
To chase the Monsters away,

Trial by fire.

WE BELONG DEAD!

And even though the laboratory where it all started

May be blown to pieces and crumble to the ground,
All it takes is just one electrical impulse
For the Monster to return.
The same Monster, who led your children to the waters of revelry
And unknowingly threw them in – to rebellion.
Remembering as a kid how bad I wanted to be Batman,
But grew up to be Emotional Dracula,
Sucking the life out everything and everyone around me.
Unable to even look myself in the mirror.
Remaining in solitude from the sunlight.
Taking chemicals to make me Invisible to the World.
Panic! At the Opera – Phantom of the Disco.
Mad – Raving til dawn with all of the night children,

O WHAT MUSIC THEY MAKE!

And no, I'm not a killer but don't push me –
No harm shall befall you lest you try removing this mask –
This FAÇADE to hide my true horrible nature
From a world that can never love me.
The gifts of sobriety also housing these curses:
These feelings – These feelings that I had locked away –
Had entombed – Sealed up in Golden Shrine Sarcophagi.
Feelings I spent so long burying deep, deep away from the world.
Until one day, some asshole comes along and digs it all up…
Unintentionally disturbing this centuries long rest,
Asking for a cigarette at the bus stop.
And force me, once again, to be resurrected –
In gauze bandage dressings of old wounds.
Force me, once again, to walk amongst the living –
To Walk like an Egyptian,
Wrapped up in all my self-righteous Bullshit!
But still every Monster demands its mate.
Reincarnations of Ancient Love –
Ankh-es-en-Eamon – Scroll of Thoth.
My Egyptian Princess.
My return to this world is only for your sake.

MY LOVE FOR YOU HAS LASTED LONGER THAN THE TEMPLE OF OUR GODS.

But with every needle I stuck into my vein
Like a stake driven into my heart –
No matter how many Coors Light Silver Bullets
Combined with handfuls of sleeping pills,
When all I wanted was just to die
And be rid of this beast I had become.
But after every attempt, always awakened for another sick sequel –
But for what? – The entertainment of others?
To be another cog in a corporate machine,
Brought back time after time to make the Studio money.

Why can't they just let this Wolf-Man die?!
But No! – No more. I refuse!
I have played the role of victim long enough.
Marked for death with Pentagram vision on hand –

Because even a man who is pure in heart
And says his prayers by night,
Knows not what lies waiting on darkened paths
Obscured from the Full Moon's light.

Something worse than foggy graveyards and cobweb crypts.
Something ghastlier than cliché Jekyll/Hyde Complex.
Something scarier than comical Abbott/Costello Encounters.
It's something that lays waiting in abandoned Traphouse Castles:
It's sleeping in the dirt and waking up in boxes.
Nosferatu! Undead Spirit!
You poor, misinformed fools– All of you!
Thinking that your Garlic necklaces can keep you safe
From the terror that awaits!
All of these horror stories,
Tales told around 12 Step campfires.
Submitted for the approval of the Midnight Society...
The most terrifying thought of all,
Is this Monster someday returning.
Because you know how it works in the movies...
They come back…
They *ALWAYS* come back.

Troy, July 2018

CONTENTS

POST-ACUTE WITHDRAWAL SOLILOQUY

The Tao is flowing against me…
Ready to crash down with the force of a massive tidal wave.
Bracing myself for it to hit me,
Like that first cold burst of water
When you turn on the showers in Jail…
Shall I always remain Jon Snow,
The bastard child,
Being sent to this wall of my own creation?
Stacked endlessly in every direction, All in All,
With Bricks of Guilt, and Pain, and Devastation.
Plastered with Anxiety,
On a solid foundation of Depression. Desperation.
Made with no Architecture Major –
We Don't Need No Education!
In this structure they can't break.
Things feel structured, things feel safe.
2:30 and 10:30 Lock-Ins. 3 Hots and a Cot.
A prisoner of my own Devices,
Only I control the lock.
Numb in comfort in this Box.
Numbers I can call Collect.
Is There Anybody Out There?
I'm starting to forget.
Calling out when I feel helpless,
But when I call Nobody's Home.
IS THERE ANYBODY OUT THERE?!
"Your Call Was Not Accepted"... (Dial Tone)
Why do I always come here to get away,
When all I really want is not to feel so alone?
But Out There everything's unsure.
Out There everything's unknown.
Out There, Beyond the Wall, they say The Others roam…
Coming up asking for change.
Out There it's DSS, SNAP, TANF,
$163 a Month, Tom Petty Cash.
The Waiting is the Hardest Part.
R.I.P. to my P.N.A.
Out There dense clouds of emotion form from my apathy,
And I'm the Lightning Rod in a Drama Storm.
What's the forecast Sexy Weather Girl?
A Torrential Downpour of paperwork and appointments:

Catch the 11:44 Under the Bridge.
Red Hot Chili Pepper Speedball.
Poli-ticking Paris Climate Change Time Bomb,
Trump's pullout game is weak.
And when it comes to putting up walls
He obviously doesn't have shit on me!
Broken promises. Broke and in need.
Broken pipes and syringes flood the streets;
Schenectady Sanitation couldn't keep us addicts clean.
As the sirens, fireworks, and ignorant people scream –
Can't find a Peaceful place to sleep, or read
Or even THINK!...
They smoke Loud because quiet don't exist in this City.
And Out There, things aren't always as they seem…
Roofie Pill Pudding Pop.
Bill Cosby Benadryl Dream.
Out There Cash Rules Everything Around Me
C.R.E.A.M! But I'm   Asset
                     Limited
                     Income
                     Constrained
                     Employed in Wonderland.
        And *We're All, Mad, Here.*
Out There we end up broken when coming off the Wall –
Humpty Dumpty Dark Knight.
Bruce, Why Do We Fall?
And All the King's Horses, and All the King's Men
Can't ever make the pieces quite fit right again –
Potato Head Picasso Portrait Mode.
Out There I can't find Service.
Out There it's always Buffering.
My senses have started returning
And I see the world is suffering.
So I Meditate for 40 years under the Tree of Knowledge.
The Serpent tells me to eat its fruit,
And I feel Shameful and Exposed.
And the Fear that I will fail
Is the snake that eats its tail.
I don't believe. And that is why.
Out There, it's "*Do* or *Do Not.*
There Is No *Try.*"
Out There I search for answers
But all I ever get is questioned.

But Why?

Why have to answer to anything but a Higher Calling

When I stopped answering the Call to get High?

Outside this Pandora's Box where I'm confined

I have to limp forward without a crutch now to face my Demons,

But my Spirit Gate is closed.

Out There are roads paved with Good Intentions,

But Out There I feel lost without direction.

No GPSes, when you hit bottom

At least there's nowhere to go but up –

Up this Stairway to Heaven.

I take 8 Steps forward, 10 Steps back,

12 Step Programs and Repentance.

Acceptance – We'll Keep Coming Back

"After a Brief Word from Our Sponsors" –

Count your Blessings, Do the Step Work,

Ain't No - Half Steppin'.

Wanna go for a run, like Forrest Gump,

But the Justice System has me tethered.

Drug Court Dates and UDSes,

Call my Color, Gotta Pee, like I drank 15 Dr. Peppers...

But maybe if I pass them all, and maybe if I pray:

"Dear God. Make me a bird. To fly far, far away."

While Lynyrd Skynyrd plays,

I'll be Free as a Bird and This Bird You Cannot Change!

Yes! Free At Least. Free At Last!

Free the Nipple. Free Bus Pass –

Oh The Places We Will Go...

The nightmares our future's hold

Will be dreams compared to our pasts.

And That's All,

     I Got To Say,

          About That.

Purcell House, June 2017

HOT GIRL AT DRUG COURT

Your eyes, for a moment, met with mine…

But you were looking at seven years jail time.

OoOoO you're a bad girl, huh?

Fiery haired wicked angel.

Sweet Shiva — Goddess of self-destruction.

Love skeletons in your bedroom's closet.

Junk withdrawal — Suffering — Sadness.

Let me be the spike in your vein,

That takes all your pain away.

Bus 370 from Troy to Schenectady

September 7, 2017

FORECAST

What's the Forecast Sexy Weather Girl?*
> I wake up to your pretty face every Morning.
> You're usually the best News of the day.

What's the Forecast Sexy Weather Girl?
> You clear away the overcast skies.
> I'd like to give you a Warm Front
> And make your Dew Point rise.

What's the Forecast Sexy Weather Girl?
> **LIES! LIES! LIES!**
> Bad News. Bad News. Fake News Networks –
> Left-Leaning Political Propaganda appropriated for our palates!
> More Genetically Modified Mindfood for Breakfast.

What's the Forecast Sexy Weather Girl?
> Around-the-clock Manic thought process –
> Brain is a spiraling Fidget-Spinner.
> My Crown Chakra hasn't bloomed in weeks,
> I'm in bad soil.

What's the Forecast Sexy Weather Girl?
> Merry Melody Mozart Motown Morning Meditations.
> 6 AM Blissful Backyard Solitude.

What's the Forecast Sexy Weather Girl?
> LOUD! LOUD! LOUD Electric City Mid-day Mayhem!
> Traffic tears through Concrete Jungle screaming.
> The Tower roars with the pain of poverty.

What's the Forecast Sexy Weather Girl?
> Tequila Sunrise. Dark Side of Moon.
> Total Eclipse of All – Human – Decency.

What's the Forecast Sexy Weather Girl?
> Cold and Flu Season.
> Jailhouse Cup-A-Soup for the Soulless.

What's the Forecast Sexy Weather Girl?
> God's wrath on Miami –
>> Mexico –
>> Madness.

What's the Forecast Sexy Weather Girl?
> Apocalypse Now? Or in the next 7 days?
> The Ring. The Eye of the Hurricane.
> The Horror…
> *The Horror.*

What's the Forecast Sexy Weather Girl?
> Irma pounding Keys like Ray Charles crazy Jazz Hands!
> I want to *Spirit Finger*[1] the hottest junkie in the Meeting…

---

[1] *"Spirit Fingers"* are an indication used by the chairperson at some 12-Step Meetings, which alert the person sharing that they have strayed away from the topic of discussion.

No Greg, stop it! That's *GETTING OFF,* topic.
What's the Forecast Sexy Weather Girl?
Nuns with chainsaws.
Fallen trees.
Pumpkin Spice Everything.
What's the Forecast Sexy Weather Girl?
Rain Drop.
Drop Top.
Fragile Fabergé Eggshell Ego –
How easily my pride can shatter in sobriety.
What's the Forecast Sexy Weather Girl?
Struck by a Bolt of Lightning.
Effects of Chemical Mixtures.
Kid Flash – My Speed Force
Was a 90mg-a-day Adderall habit,
And a past I can never seem to outrun.
What's the Forecast Sexy Weather Girl?
Lovers lying in grassy shade beneath the sunbathed treetops.
To walk hand and hand through the storm.
To kiss passionately in a downpour.
To imagine the delicate warm embrace of your body against mine
Until my peaceful thoughts are once again interrupted
By somebody on the bus, complaining about Trump.
What's the Forecast?
Stormy Daniels, Stormy Daniels.
Russia, Russia. Blah, Blah, Blah…
I'm not saying I always agree with what our President does,
I'm just so SICK of hearing about it every time I turn on the TV,
When all I want to do is watch Teen Titans Go!
What's the Forecast Sexy Weather Girl?
Dancing around Drum Circle –
Blazing Sage sanctifying spirits–
Sacred sexual ceremonies –
Showing the Native girl my Smudge Stick.
What's the Forecast Sexy Weather Girl?
Killer Clowns and deep seeded Childhood Traumas.
A beautiful October day in Derry,
And I'm Lactose Intolerant.
What's the Forecast Sexy Weather Girl?
Destruction of Sodom.
My beautiful Gamora.
Let me be your Star-Lord.
Come and Get Your Love.
What's the Forecast Sexy Weather Girl?
ComiCon Cosplay Contentment.
Cool Autumn Morning.
January Embers.
Light freckled skin marked by the kisses
Of a thousand Sun Gods...
Oh those lucky, lucky Sun Gods.

What's the Forecast Sexy Weather Girl?
> The clinicians at Outpatient keep hiring
> All these good-looking Interns.
> So when do I get to start working there?

WEATHER UPDATE:
SINCE THIS POEM WAS ORIGINALLY WRITTEN,
I ACTUALLY HAVE BECOME AN INTERN AT MY OLD OUTPATIENT…
NOW <u>THAT</u> GOES TO SHOW YOU THE POWER OF INTENTION!

What's the Forecast?
> Sexy Nubian Queens –
> Caramel Cleopatra Smiling at me
> In Samarian Indian-Summer Sunlight.

What's the Forecast?
> Beautiful Bronze statuesque bodies
> In line at banks or boarding buses –
> You going my way Light and Sweet thang?
> You KNOW how I like my coffee –
> And damn all of you white boys
> Taking all our Beautiful Black Women!

…Forecast
> The house down the street always smells like Piff.

What's the Forecast Sexy Weather Girl?
> What the fuck is happening to the world?
> It feels like I'm chained to the radiator
> While the building burns down around me.

So what's the Forecast Sexy Weather Girl?
> My Pink Clouds are gathering on the horizon.
> So please grant us one more luminous Dawn,
> With a 50 percent chance of Peace and Love.
> Show us one more 5 Day Forecast
> Of Sunny Symbols across our Screens…

My Sweet Sexy Weather Girl.

Schenectady, October 2017

*The "Sexy Weather Girl" mentioned throughout this poem is both a metaphor and in actuality the sexy weather girl from Channel 6 News that I would see on TV every morning when I was in the Halfway House

KILLER FROST

She is Sweet Melody

 Of both Fire and Ice.

Diving deep into the Glacial Pools of those cool

 Blue Eyes that Chill me to the bone.

Beauty that hits me like Arctic Air

 Traveling on Western Winds.

12,799 Miles of Lonely Earth rolling between us.

At times, I can feel your pain, from a country away.

Raging Wild Winter Fire,

 California Girl – My Khaleesi –

  I, am the Dragon. And you, are my Princess.

Moon of my Life – My Sun and Stars.

 The Universe displayed its aptitude for Art,

  On the night, it drew the two of us together.

Schenectady
November 9, 2017

WHAT A WORLD

These streets have become a desolate wasteland…
Just look around – Look and see.
See what has become of us.
Lone Elders downtrodden and tattered –
Pushing shopping cart down sidewalks,
Picking empty notebooks from wastebaskets.
Used pens and textbook pages litter lawns.
The education addict nods off outside the Library doors,
Waiting for it to open, to go inside and get more.
Rich Men clad in Business Suits – Standing on corners
Begging for change – To Social Policies.
"Get some Public Assistance ya fuckin bum!" I sharply snap back at him.
Social Workers and Clinicians lurking in parks and alleyways –
"Hey man, wanna try some Recovery? All the cool kids are doing it," They say.
Teenage boys hiding Daily Devotional magazines under mattresses.
Young girl caught on her knees in private… Punished for praying.
Children dressed in Hazmat suits, for fear of oxytocin exchange, from embrace.
People forced to walk with surgical masks on their faces –
Because they know that smiles are contagious.
The Bando across the street is an Animal Traphouse –
The Pigs have been knocking at the door 3 times today
But the Big Bad Wolf won't let them in.
Beavers building bridges out of Dental Dams.
There are Cats on the porch all day getting high on catnip –
Looking for an angry fix… Of Meow Mix.
A rabid Raccoon is pacing on the roof with a 40 and a pack of Newports –
The Police openly discriminate and target anybody who has black...
Rimmed glasses –
And will NOT hesitate to shoot when you reach for your Diplomas!
I desperately try finding a way to escape this madness –
Looking for sanctuary,
I duck into hole-in-the-wall Church basement –
Greeted with a handshake, a hug, and a chip.
And suddenly surrounded by people saying:
"Join us... Join us... Join us – in the Fellowship"…
I jet the hell out of there for my life, running back into the streets screaming:
"WHAT HAVE I DONE TO DESERVE ALL THESE BLESSINGS!!!"
An Ambulance screeches up – EMS strapping me down onto gurney –
Feverishly trying to resuscitate me from an overdose of Philosophy,
Poetry, Coffeehouse Jazz, and Arts & Crafts.
I come to sweaty, shaking, and sick in a Jail Cell – In the middle of a tornado –
I look out the window and Community Residence Director flies by on broomstick
Cackling: *"I'll get you my pretty... And your cat can't come with you!"*

I click the heels of my orange Jail Crocs together 3 times repeating:
"There's no place like Halfway House.
　　　There's no place like Halfway House.
　　　　There's no place like Halfway House."
I wake up from this nightmare surrounded by smiling familiar faces.
I just had the craziest dream – And you were there –
And you – And you – And all of you!
Washed clean by the waters of Recovery –
Sent from misguided bucket aimed for a Scarecrow,
The worst parts of me Melting –
　　　　　　Melting –
　　　　　　　Melting away.

What a World! What. A. World…

Schenectady/Troy, April 2017

NIGHTHAWK

The Nighthawk comes to visit me once again –
Looming large on my Nightstand
Watching me till Daybreak.
Carrying messages of Terror tied to its leg.
Flying in through the burst open shutters of my Soul.
The Nighthawk is vivid Nicotine Patch Nightmare.
The Nighthawk sits pecking at my Pineal Gland.
The Nighthawk keeps my eyelids pried open in its claws –
Staring at the screen of my phone.
The Nighthawk is endless mental To-Do Lists
Playing Duck-Duck-Goose during my Meditation.
The Nighthawk is missing Yoga Group –
Unable to practice Pigeon Pose.
The Nighthawk is long loud
Late-night bus ride on 905
Trying to read Lao Tzu –
Just let me off on Lark.
The Nighthawk is Buzzard screech cars in the street
Burning out tires at 12 AM.
The Nighthawk is roommate Boombox blasting
Awful Rap that's always yapping,
Crap-rap-rapping inside our chamber door.
When I'd rather not a peeping,
For you see when I am sleeping,
If there's any sound that's pleasing
Classical Music I implore –
But alas… Quoth the Nighthawk:

> ♫ *Little bitch you can't fuck with me, if you wanted to!*
> *This expensive. These is red bottoms.*
> *These is bloody shoes!* ♫

Could you PLEASE turn that SHIT OFF!?

Where Have You Gone to Lauryn Hill?
How I miss That Thing, That Thing you did.
Where have you flown Sweet Songbird?
I see the void you've left in your absence.
Shallow – And now only filled with
Silicone and Human Compost…

The Nighthawk is ravenous Rooster call alarms –
Rousing me awake like a punch in the face.
The Nighthawk is Community Residence Mama-Bird
Pushing me from the nest and expecting me to fly.
No more Halfway-Home-for-the-Holidays.
Psyche snapping at the Shopping Mall.

Nightmare on 6th Avenue
Before Christmas.
  9.
     10...
         Never.
            Sleep.
                 Again.
The Nighthawk is a circling flock
Of Department Store Seagulls in Parking Lots
Waiting to descend upon their Target.
The Nighthawk shaves its head Bald
And masquerades as the symbol of Freedom.
Unable to keep a steady Right Wing.
Perched on 3 Branches of Government Shutdown –
You should know the Nighthawk doesn't stand for Dreamers!
The Nighthawk's Left-Wing spreading propaganda.
Regurgitating lies into little Liberal mouths
That Tweet incessantly, starving – For attention.
The Nighthawk is needlessly nay-saying Newscasters –
Squawking on every Station.
Shut up and show the Weather Girl!
Nuclear Postcards from North Korea – Wish You Were Here.
Atomic Blondes and Ice Cream. Chocolate Chip Cookie Death!
Brown Sugar sprinkles. All us victims to the Spoon –
But all they bitch about is Russia!
Neunundneunzig Luftballons!
They Ruffle their Feathers and get all tumultuous.
But Hillary lost; can't you get the fuck over it?!
I guess half of you don't even know
What it's like to be *actually* "Woke"…
Because the Nighthawk is Democrats picking bits
Of flesh from the bones of School Shooting victims –
Never let a tragedy go to waste for Politics.
Birds of Prey preparing to pillage your Desert Eagles.
While all the birds in Schenectady fly
Southeast to shit all over Liberty Street.
The Emperor Penguin places a Crack Rock
At the Hood Rat's feet and they mate for life.
The Nighthawk is this Criminal Pigeonholed past –
Committed to continue walking on Eggshells
Or be left looking like the Cat that ate the Canary.
Treatment Court throwing me back in my cage.
I guess I'll always just be a Jailbird.
The Nighthawk is 6 AM Med Calls
Monday Morning Med Lines
Or Metal Doors Buzzing.
Breakfast Tray Delivery
During TB Test Solitary.
Confined to thin hard cot.
One of many Mitochondria

Marching through metal detectors to Medical.
Another one-celled organism under Justice System Microscope –
And All the World's A Stage.
So don't let this be my Swan Song…
The Nighthawk is Coffee at 9 PM,
Heavy Workloads, Heavy Backpack Pain.
I'll be a Shrugged Atlas,
The weight of World History Textbooks resting on my shoulders.
My neck is killing me from carrying everything on my mind!
The Nighthawk is 10 Page Term Papers,
Tests, and Technological distraction...
Hi, my name is Greg
And I'm a Tinder Addict.
Having to steal Wi-Fi at the Halfway House
Just to make a connection.
"I don't think Leonard can hack it".
By the way in case you didn't catch it
That was a reference to Full Metal Jacket…
Damn and I still have these four Chapters
Left to read for classes,
But oh shit, I just got three more Matches!
Wait, what was I doing again?
Oh yeah, a poem, that's right…

But still either way at the end of the night
I'll just be heading home alone again,
At curfew to an empty bed.
Yup just me and my Nighthawk...
A lot of these girls here at Treatment are cute
I don't want to be a Vulture though...
But sometimes I feel like a Birdwatcher
Just looking for some Swallow or Great Tits –
And yes, those are actually names of Birds,
Just so you know…
But in all seriousness though, despite
All the things that keep me up at Night,
At Dawn, the Nighthawk flies away.
And it's waking up clean just one more day
That makes it worth getting out of bed
Every Morning.

Troy, April 2018

"IF THAT PLANE LEAVES THE GROUND AND YOU'RE NOT WITH HIM, YOU'LL REGRET IT…" (OR: "WE'LL ALWAYS HAVE HAMPTON MANOR")

I believe some remnants
  Of My Heart still remain –
On the underside of the Garbage Disposal
  Into which it was poured,
From that Blender on the Kitchen Counter
  Of some Girl's house back in
    East Greenbush.

My Soul, is on a piece of paper –
  Probably still in some drawer
  Or a Shoebox –
After selling it to a Friend
  Sometime back in 2004 –
    For a Beef Patty
      And a Cigarette.

My Life that I sacrificed
  To Heroin –
Pierced through the Flesh –
  Crucified on a Cross of
Diabetic Insulin Needles –
  3rd Day Naloxone Resurrection.

But what none of them actually knows,
  Is they only accepted the fakes –
The real ones I hide,
  Here in my mind,
    Where nobody ever can take.

Still Point Retreat Center
August 25, 2018

MY NATURE

"I'm not used to being in Nature"
   Is what comes to mind as I stand here at Still Point
   Staring up into space – Feeling somewhat out of place.
I'm not used to being in Nature –
I'm not used to such sounds of silence.
   Not even in my own mind.
I'm used to 3 AM neighbor screaming matches,
Screeching tires, and Fire and Rescue sirens –
   I'm not used to this.
You see, I'm not used to being in Nature –
   The only R and R I get is Rehab and Running
   From Bus Stop to Bus Stop, From Classes to Court.
   The fear of prison system Recidivism Rates.
   May I not be another Statistic.
Because Nature for me isn't spiritually serene –
   It's Wine and Spirits stores on every street,
   The Homeless and Hustlers on every corner.
My Nature isn't Campfires and S'mores or Sleeping Bags and Tents –
   My Nature is Dopesick and Poor and Sleeping on a Bench,
   Or Slumlord random stop-bys since you're still late on the rent.
My Nature is Back Alley littered with broken furniture and mattresses.
   Garbage Bag Tumbleweeds blowing in the breeze.
My Nature is big dogs barking behind fences at everyone that passes,
   Squirrels tearing through all the trashes, and of course
   The Raccoon in the Backyard who ran up on our porch
   For a pack of Newports and snatched it…
   I can't make this kinda shit up by the way,
   Cause that ACTUALLY HAPPENED!
My Nature isn't Row Boats, Fishing, Rope Swings and Swimming Holes –
My Nature is the polluted pond in a lower class Suburban Neighborhood
   That hasn't been safe to swim in since I was six.
My Nature is a Wilderness of Concrete, Steel,
And Red Brick Low Income Housing Developments –
   The unknown, which lies in the Jungle
   Of the abandoned building's lawn next door,
   That hasn't been mowed in 5 months.
My Nature is crowded Cell Block Summer Camp –
   I'll be locked in at 10 o'clock in "Cabin #206."
So as I look around at the forests and farms – I'm not used to all of this…
I'm not used to being in Nature – In case I haven't made that clear,
I'm not used to being in Nature.
But I guess it's better than being here...

Hudson Mohawk Supportive Living
Lansingburgh
August 27, 2018

PET DETECTIVE

The writing's on the wall –
I see Missing Cat Posters all over the neighborhood.
On telephone poles, in store windows, in Libraries.
And I wonder where our furry feline friends have gone…
With no woods to explore
Or wild predators in our midst –
Where do all the runaway cats go,
Out here in the big, big city?
I believe something sinister is at play –
What fate has befallen these Collar City creatures?
I just hope they didn't run into that killer, Curiosity.
Cause you'd be hard-pressed to hope the best
Has eventually worked out for these missing pets –
That maybe they went off to Cat College
Chasing Bachelor's Degrees in Business.
Becoming Bankers and Wall Street Corporate Fat Cats.
Clad in Top Hat, Bow Tie, and Monocle.
Gathered around Dinner Tables
With shouts of "Indubitably my Good Man!"
Over a large spread of Caviar and Fancy Feast.
But no, that can't always be the case.
Maybe only for the 1%.
So what really becomes of society's Lost Pets?
I think this warrants further investigation…

Business was slow, but that's where she enters the picture –
This beautiful blond dame comes walking into my office:
Black dress and veiled hat, a long tipped cigarette holder
Resting between the fingers of her black gloved hands.
She sat across the desk from me, crossing her soft long legs;
And God I wanted her right then and there, but I had to be professional –
"Sure sweetheart, I'll help you find your kitty cat".
I poured us each a Highball – *"Here's Lookin at You Kid"* –
As she gave me the low down on this troubled Tabby,
Missing since August 18th –
You see, his Mother was a Minx… A real Wildcat.
She used to sneak out to prowl the streets in Heat,
Letting any mangy beast have their way with her.
Until one day, she found herself knocked up.
And the Father, not ready to raise a kitten,
Took the first train to Splitsville, see?
And stopped returning her Cat Calls.
Now stuck with a litter she couldn't support,
She had to stay in a Subsidized Cat Shelter
And apply for Cat Food Stamps –
A real sad case indeed.
Now our Tabby was the runt of the bunch,

Always found himself fighting for food.
So once he started growing up things got a little rough –
He dropped out of Obedience School and got mixed up
With a group of Bad Kitties on the East Side.
And at the time, there was tension between breeds,
So every day was Cat Fight.
One night, when the claws came out,
He even lost an ear in a back alley rumble
With the Black Cats that claimed territory
On the block back towards Home.
He had a run-in with the Police Dogs,
For Pawed Robbery of a Fish Market,
And got put in the Pound.
The Judge released him on Parole.
Told him keep his mitts clean – Easy enough, right?
But this Town can be one giant Litter Box...
Now the Tabby started spending time at the local Scratching Post,
And got caught up with some Cool Kittens
That performed Jazz and knew how to Scat –
  Because a Cat's the Only Cat
    Who Knows Where it's At –
Man I hear those Cats could really wail!
But he ended up with a pretty nasty Nip habit, dig?
Went back to the Kennel since he wasn't no Rat –
And that was before things really got bad...

So word on the street was our Tabby here
Grew partial to placing bets on the Boxers –
He took a 50 to 1 shot on this Underdog from a False Tip
That his opponent would throw the Bone in the next big Dog Fight –
But he really Screwed the Pooch on that one!
Got 20 Large deep with a mean pack of Persians.
Now that's quite a bit of Scratch –
And the last thing you want to be
Is in a bad batch of Meow-Mix with the Mob.
So our boy had to take a Flee Bath, if you know what I mean,
Skip town and *Brush* them off before the situation got too *Hairy*
And they sent some Maine Coon Goons to *Hack* off his *Furrballs*!
So the police put him in Witness Protection,
Gave him the name "Mittens", and placed him in the care
Of the beautiful young lady sitting here across from me –
And now we're almost up to speed.
Our Tabby finally had a Home,
An owner, and was happy;
And everything was not too shabby –
Or so it seemed…
See, you can take the Cat out of the Hood
But can't take the Hood out of the Cat –
So one night he just disappeared.
Did he go back? Damn, where's he at?

Did the Mob somehow manage to follow in his tracks?
Or did the Nip come back calling?
Was he off getting high,
In a tree that he climbed,
And couldn't find his way back down,
From fear of falling?
No clues for where he went,
But I know I'll get him back –
So time to get out on the case
And get my suitcase packed –
You know the usual things:
A bag of treats, a squeaky mouse,
A fishing pole toy with a feather on a string.

So has your furry pal run off and become a member
Of the dark recesses of the animal underworld?
Is that pussy stuck... In a basement or a dumpster?
Did your kitty up and hit the skids?
Well that's where I come in…
Just call me! –
Greg Wilder...
Pet Detective.

Troy, September 2018

IT Comes Back

IT came back…
Approaching 8 Months since the tragedy –
To be honest, I had nearly forgotten.
Not sure what sparks the memory back now,
Staring out the window on this cold, gray October morning –
When my feelings start to mirror the changing of the seasons,
And the summer slowly fades away to fall.
That nip in the air and deteriorating Sunlight.
As the piling leaves stripped from their branches
Brings to mind the barrenness of the trees,
And how they seem to mimic the emptiness
Of impending S.A.D.ness in the months to come…
Or maybe with Halloween on the horizon,
Horror hangs more heavily in the air.
And here I stand, a Bipolar Santa Claus,
On the eve of winter's first snowfall –
And all is well on the North Pole of course,
      Until all you do, is give and give,
          And then things go South,
              And *IT* comes back…
IT always comes back – When you least expect it.
IT creeps up when you're at your most vulnerable.
IT knows your every weakness.
IT keeps you paralyzed in your bed.
IT is your worst Nightmares come to life
At every waking moment,
Afraid to get up and face the day ahead.
IT plays on your every Fear and Anxiety:
That everyone is against you.
That your life is all a lie.
Telling you you'll never be good enough,
So what's the point to try?
IT is my two failed suicide attempts
And every time someone else succeeds –
So sometimes, I wonder
Why I'm still here…
When *IT* drags our children into the deep –
With promises of Balloons and Floating.

A Journal Entry:
Saturday, March 10, 2018 –
IT claimed another victim this morning…
Police pulled the body from the River –
An old friend of mine – I found out while walking around the Mall.

A feeling of intense numbness washing over me –
As if the perpetrator crept up from behind,
Looking over my shoulder laughing.
Knowing this was *IT*s doing –
The Sadness and Anger and Disgust,
At the town that we come from.
A place, which to me is a manifestation of *IT*.
And how, after all this time, did I manage to forget?
Maybe I've just been too busy –
Too caught up in the riff raff
Of rat race responsibilities to stop and think.
Too busy Adulting – Too busy running from my past,
To allow *IT* to all catch up with me…
Maybe it was just until now that the fear
Of having to go back makes it perfectly clear –
Because as soon as I approach the City Limits,
IT all comes flooding back…

IT comes back while thinking of turbulent teenage years –
Reminiscing… A return to this Hometown Hell.
Coming face to face with that old life you escaped.
IT was that first fateful Summer here: The Flood.
The pain of being jumped by thugs and unrequited love.
IT is the hurt person that I had become
Who just couldn't help hurting others…
Because *IT* is the neighborhood bully's torment –
Targets of their displaced feelings
Before going home to a Stepfather's beatings.
A vicious cycle of abuse.
IT is an overbearing parent's care –
Their own childhood traumas transfused.
Suffering for the sins of the Father.
IT was my lack of all self-esteem.
IT called me Nerd, a Dork, or a Dweeb.
And *IT* would always be this way,
At least that's how it seemed…
Not knowing one day I'd find
Other people just like me.
So now I can finally say:
"I'm proud to be in The Loser's Club!"

The cool kids aren't as cool as us anyway…
And we all try our best to suppress *IT* every day –
To fill the empty feeling *IT* leaves inside us.
With drinks… With drugs…
With codependence or meaningless sex.
With Netflix binge watching
And social media downward comparisons.
With work. With money and material goods.
With rituals and religions –
All done in vain attempts at ignoring *IT*.
IT keeps working-poor whites from reaching out for help.
"You're privileged," they say. "You can't have any problems"
So paint a smile on that pasty clown-face and keep it moving –
Until they find you,
      With your wrists slit,
          In a bathtub
              When *IT* comes back…
Or maybe things will seem better,
For a moment, that is fleeting,
On a Therapist's couch or a 12 Step Meeting…
So as we stand with our hands held together
In this circle we can acknowledge,
Individually, we are too powerless to stop *IT*…
But together we can all finally beat this monster!
When *IT*'s gone and the scars of the past disappear,
We'll all have to make a pact,
To return if *IT* does –
And in the meantime just hope,
That this time, *IT* never comes back…

Troy, October 2018

Vicious Ending

On a cold February Morning
        Outside the New York City Courthouse.
Released into the care of the Mother who birthed
        And enabled my Demons - And the Horse
On which I can ride off into Eternal Night.

I can't remember if I killed her,
        And I'm not sure which was worse:
Withdrawing on the cold hard prison floor,
        Or the pain of what isn't known.
For 5 months building like the anticipation of that first dope-sick hit - Then suddenly,
        The party ends.

Only 2 Hours passed since revived from a blue-lipped oblivion
        And asking for more - I can't do this on my own. Mother, please
Fill my veins with the only love I have left in this life.
        Help me to end the suffering - Bury me in Leather.

I want to go be with Nancy.

Rensselaer
January 1, 2019

ADDICTED TO POETRY

Hi, my name is Greg,

    And I'm a Poetry Addict.

Oh how I need it.

    My body aches without it.

Like these Alexandrines are filled with Benzedrine –

    I'm addicted to Poetry.

I stay out all night

    At Open Mics,

Looking for a Poetess to go home with –

    So I can get inside her Chapbook.

I roll up Leaves of Grass on the daily.

    I'm addicted to poetry.

I tie off and then I

    Mainline Blake Rhymes,

Count the feet, but it didn't have legs. [2]

    So waking up sick I needed a hit

And then broke out the spoon and the Dickinson –

    I'm ad-dic-a-ted – To poetry.

I can't deal with life without it.

    I'm completely at a loss.

And I can't function when I wake up

    Till I crack open some Frost.

I'm a hopeless poet addict – And I don't know how to stop it –

    Doing line after line after line…

---

[2] *"Legs"* is the terminology used by heroin addicts to explain how long a specific batch will keep you high for, *"Feet"* is obviously the poetry term related to scansion. Feet – Legs. Get it? Well, if not, what the hell kind of poetry critic are you then?

        Of these Sonnets.

I'm a straight-up poem fiend – I scratch feverishly
      As I walk through the Library aisles.
Then I grab some and rush to the Bathroom,
      Get my pipe loaded packed-full of Dactyls.
Would you suck a dick for some Edgar Allan Poe?
      Well if so… Then you may be addicted to poetry!

And ever since poetry's entered my life,
      It's only been making a mess of it.
Just this week I had gotten arrested with
      A bag full of T.S. Eliot.
And as soon as the cop pulled me over
      He could already tell by the smell of it.
    *— **POEMS RUIN HOMES** —*
They tried to send me off to Rehab
      I said: NO – NO – NO!
Impossible! I'm fine! That's right!
      I can End-Stop any time I'd like!
But when they asked me: *Can I Kick It?*
      I got the urge to try and find a mic.

My entire life is in shambles,
      And there's only one way I can fix it.
Now that I know –
      I'm addicted to poems –
        But the First Step is just to admit it.

Rensselaer, January 2019

You are the light that shines through all of life's darkness.

You are the essence. A reflection of all that is magnificent –

You are Majesty. You are Divinity.

You are true beauty Manifested –

You are Art and Music made flesh.

You are Poetry in Motion –

You are Daughters and Sisters and Aunts.

You are Mothers and Creators. You are Nature.

You are Teachers of Tribes –

Where men bring up your children to be fighters.

But Wisdom is passed down Matriarchal lines –

They say it takes a village to raise a child,

But only a Woman can turn a boy into a man!

You were the Salt of the Earth until they uprooted you.

Pulled you deep from within the African ground,

To ship and sell you across seas –

They melted you and broke you down,

To your most basic elements,

To make you fit their moulds.

They hammer and pound you into what they see as suitable shapes –

And revert you from your natural states,

Into watches and plates or rings and bracelets,

To place you into their boxes to display in well-lit cases.

They wear you out in public on their arms or necks –

To show ownership and status.

Something pretty to take home

And place on their mantelpieces.

Drug addicts breaking in to take you away –

To sell off at Bodegas and Pawn Shops

For far less than your worth in weight.

They shoot each other in the streets

In jealous rages just to possess you.

They covet you in cold carelessness.

Waging war over you wealth.

To be Woman – To be doers of every thankless job –

In a world that never puts down the toilet seat.

But there were days you adorned the walls of temples and palaces –

You were Queens and Pharaohs and Goddesses!

But they tried to suppress your Sainthoods –

They buried your Gospels and slandered your names.

They cast their stones. They toss their shade.

But no matter what they throw at you it takes

Much more than that to make true diamonds break.

So though they may call you crazy for it – Shine on!

Earth Mothers holding the seeds of existence within your wombs.

Shine on you Wonder Women, Xena Weekend Warriors!

Shine on you Rockstar Unicorn Princesses!

Shine on Liz Taylors and Countesses alike – Shine on Feminine Energy!

Shine on Androgyny! Shine on across every Gender Spectrum! –

Shine on sacred Squaws, Witches, and great Mystical Medicine Women!

Shine on Isises, Lilliths, and Aphrodites!

Shine on Strippers and Prostitutes and Porn Stars!

Shine on Virgin Maries and Single-Mother Theresas –

Elizabethan Queens with no need for kings.

Shine on Sextons, Angelous, Dickinsons, and Plaths!

Girls of Science Technology Engineering and Math!

Shine on Sexy Weathergirls – May your future Forecasts

Call for bright sunny days,

To show the world your sparkle…

You are the treasures that wait

Somewhere over Rainbows –

And you don't have to be Dorothy,

   Rose, Sophia, or Blanche

   To be Golden Girls – It's true.

So just shine on and stay gold.

All that glitters is you…

Schenectady, April 2019

A DROWNING MAN

"We, in our turn, sought the same escape with all the desperation of drowning men."

- The Big Book of Alcoholics Anonymous pg. 28

The Temptation to drown is all around.
    To nosedive into shallow ends
    Of Liquor Pools with no Lifeguards.
The Temptation to drown is all around.
    To let go and sink back to my bottom
    When the weight of the world drags me down.
    To never come up for air again.
The Temptation to drown is all around.
    I already drowned once before – Sometime in the early 90s,
    I think I was 5 – When I fell off the Fun Noodle
    After crossing the rope in our Apartment Complex pool –
    I guess you can say that was the day
    I first went off the Deep End –
    And though I survived – Only to die
    And come back again, time after time,
    Like a mask-less Jason Voorhees
    On an Amphetamine-fueled rampage,
The Temptation to drown is still around.
    When my 2-year coin doesn't double as a life preserver –
    I'm sure it would sink as fast as I can –
    Trapped inside vicious circles of condensation
    Gathered on tables –
The Temptation to drown is all around:
    Every street is paved in Black Tar Heroin.
    Every corner a sharp edge I must avoid –
    The tips of rigs poised to pierce my skin.
    Every church is a block from the Knock Spot.
    There's Panic! In Needle Park – I Pray for the Wicked –
Lead us not into Temptation – to drown.
    But I can't trust a soul –
    Every face that I breeze past
    Starts to look like a Relapse:
    A six pack of Henry's Hard Soda
    Sits at the Bus Stop, waiting
    To board the next 40 oz. Eastbound –
    To Freedom.
    Empty bottles with scratched off labels
    Shuffle into basement meetings

And call themselves "Anonymous".
While a run-down looking bottle of Rum
Is in the alleyway taking a *leak*.
(I think he may have a **CRACK** problem)
A fifth of E&J is playing chess
Against a bottle of Smirnoff in the park.
Mini-Bar bottles riding Merry Go Rounds –
All it takes is just one little push…
The Temptation to drown is all around.
Beautiful bikini-clad bottles on Beaches –
Sexy under clear blue summer skies.
Spin the Bottle – Spin the Bottle,
Kiss your life, Goodbye.
The Temptation to drown is all around.
College campuses and classrooms
Crammed with Cognacs and Coors.
Another case of Coronas caught crossing the border –
I hear they all got thrown in the Cooler…
This always happens during ICE raids.
Jaeger Bombs over Baghdad!
Wine bottle skyscrapers
Span the City skylines.
I see Constellations in the stars,
Of the scars along the crooks of my arms,
And every block must have great cell service
Cause it's never too hard to find Bars!

Temptations
To Drown
To take the plunge
Where that little plume of blood
In the needle becomes
The Mushroom Cloud
That completely destroys
Everyone…

DEVASTATION!
My adolescence filled with Butterfly Effect blackouts –
Entire Weekends Lost from Memory to Madness.
From Tequila Sunrise to Blue Moon.
These Days of Wine and Roses last too long –
And are covered with thorns.

DESPARATION!
Destroying the house in search of
That last one you're sure you hid.
Diving into dumpsters.
Tearing through trash bags
For some empties to scrape…
All I need is enough for just one little taste.

DELERIUM!
"A Disease of the Night" –
The sweating. The shaking.
The raving, screaming hallucinations:
Little Animals! Lions and Tigers and Bitter Ends –
Jails, Institutions, and Death
OH MY!
Trapped in the Halfway House Heartbreak Hotel.
Fear and Loathing in Lansingburgh.
Say It Ain't So!
My Pink Cloud Bursteth…
A storm of Life on Life's Terms.

So, here I am…
    1,000 Days in Sobriety.
    Still drunk off my own pretentiousness.
    Passed out in puddles of Word Vomit.
The Temptation will never go away,
    So I pray: God,
    Grant me the Serenity,
    To not freak out and murder
    Every last one of my enemies!
3 DUIs – But they can never take my Poetic License.
    So I'mma ride this bitch till the wheels fall off
    As I trudge the Road of Happy Destiny!
May God Bless Me – And Keep Me –
Until Then…

Schenectady
January 2020

The End

It's a
WilderCo.
Production!

© COPYRIGHT MMXX

1. "**Prologue**" contains elements from *Frankenstein (1931 Film)* Directed by James Whale

2. "**A Universal Monster**" contains elements from *Dracula (1931 Film)* Directed by Tod Browning; *Bride of Frankenstein (1935 Film)* Directed by James Whale; *The Mummy (1932 Film)* Directed by Karl Freund; and *Are You Afraid of the Dark? (1990 Television Series)* Created by D.J. MacHale and Ned Kandel

3. "**Post-Acute Withdrawal Soliloquy**" contains elements from *Forrest Gump (1994 Film)* Directed by Robert Zemeckis; *Star Wars Episode V: The Empire Strikes Back (1980 Film)* Directed by George Lucas; *Batman Begins (2005 Film)* Directed by Christopher Nolan; *Freebird (1973 Song)* Recorded by Lynyrd Skynyrd; and *C.R.E.A.M. (1993 Song)* Recorded by Wu-Tang Clan

4. "**Forecast**" contains elements from *Heart of Darkness (1902 Novel)* Written by Joseph Conrad; and *Bad and Boujee (2017 Song)* Recorded by Migos featuring Lil Uzi Vert

5. "**Killer Frost**" contains elements from *A Game of Thrones (1996 Novel)* Written by George R.R. Martin

6. "**What A World**" contains elements from *The Wizard of Oz (1939 Film)* Directed by Victor Fleming

7. "**NightHawk**" contains elements from *Bodak Yellow (2017 Song)* Recorded by Cardi B.; and *Full Metal Jacket (1987 Film)* Directed by Stanley Kubrick.

8. "**Pet Detective**" contains elements from *Casablanca (1942 Film)* Directed by Michael Curtiz

9. "**IT Comes Back**" contains elements from *IT (1986 Novel)* Written by Stephen King

10. "**Addicted to Poetry**" contains elements from *Rehab (2006 Song)* Recorded

by Amy Winehouse

11. **"A Drowning Man"** contains elements from *The Lost Weekend (1944 Novel)* Written by Charles R. Jackson; *The Serenity Prayer (1932 Sermon)* Written by Reinhold Niebuhr; and *Alcoholics Anonymous: The Story of How Many Thousands of Men and Women Have Recovered from Alcoholism (1939 Book)* Written by William "Bill W." Wilson.

AWARDS AND PUBLICATIONS

Friends of Recovery – New York 2018 Recovery Fine Arts Awards – 2nd Place, Poetry for "*What a World*"

5th Annual Stephen A. DiBiase Poetry Contest – Finalist for "*What a World*"

"*What a World*" featured in *Addiction/Recovery* (Anthology by Madness Muse Press)

"*Addicted to Poetry*" featured in "*Three Poems at CapCity Slam Open Mic Night*" (Article by Albany Times Union

"*Vicious Ending*" featured in *CAPS Poetry 2020: 20th Anniversary* (Anthology by Calling All Poets)

"*Post-Acute Withdrawal Soliloquy*" featured in 2020 Issue of *Barzakh Magazine*

"*Golden Girls*" featured in *Havik 2020* by Havik: The Las Positas College Journal of Arts and Literature

"*IT Comes Back*" will be featured in the October 2020 Issue of *Down in the Dirt Magazine* by Scars Publications

ACKNOWLEDGMENTS

Special thanks to Judith Prest: First Reader for my manuscript, a coworker, a friend, and the one who first encouraged me to continue this journey into crafting my poetry. I would also like to thank my family for supporting my dream of writing and my newfound sobriety. Thank you to the staff at New Choices Recovery Center, Judge Young and the Rensselaer County Treatment Court team, John Fox and The Institute for Poetic Medicine, Albany Poets, D. Colin and everyone at the Poetic Vibe Open Mic Night in Troy, N.Y., all of my Professors and the staff at SUNY Schenectady, my cats, and (of course) my Sponsor…

Photo Courtesy of *Robert Cooper Jr. Photography*

ABOUT THE AUTHOR

Gregory C. Wilder Jr. (also known by the stage name Slay! the Dragon) is an award-winning writer, full-time student, and spoken word poetry performer, currently residing in Schenectady, N.Y. After a long, downhill battle with alcohol and drug addiction, Greg entered treatment in June of 2017 and rediscovered the therapeutic potential of art and writing. Today, with over three years clean and while interning for a drug and alcohol treatment center, Greg now shares the healing power of poetry with other recovering addicts. Greg received an A.S. in Human Services after graduating from SUNY Schenectady in May 2020.

Made in the USA
Middletown, DE
19 August 2020

15787028R00024